T0353857

AUTISM-
A Family's Journey

FATIMA AIT BRAHIM

© 2024 Fatima Ait Brahim. All rights reserved.

No part of this book may be reproduced, stored in a retrieval system, or
transmitted by any means without the written permission of the author.

AuthorHouse™ UK
1663 Liberty Drive
Bloomington, IN 47403 USA
www.authorhouse.co.uk
UK TFN: 0800 0148641 (Toll Free inside the UK)
UK Local: 02036 956322 (+44 20 3695 6322 from outside the UK)

Because of the dynamic nature of the Internet, any web addresses or links contained
in this book may have changed since publication and may no longer be valid. The views
expressed in this work are solely those of the author and do not necessarily reflect the views
of the publisher, and the publisher hereby disclaims any responsibility for them.

Any people depicted in stock imagery provided by Getty Images are models,
and such images are being used for illustrative purposes only.
Certain stock imagery © Getty Images.

This book is printed on acid-free paper.

ISBN: 979-8-8230-8760-5 (sc)
979-8-8230-8761-2 (e)

Print information available on the last page.

Published by AuthorHouse 05/15/2024

authorHOUSE

AUTISM-

A Family's Journey

Autism Research

In this book, the causes and effects of Autism will be researched and documented. I will introduce what Autism is, causes of Autism and how to help heal your child with Autism. Also, my personal experience with my brother will be shared. The aim of this book is to give an insight to all readers what Autism is, how to manage the Autism in a child/adult and have Hope in healing through structured intervention, increased awareness and helping the world understand Autism through Autistic eyes. There's no powerful way to learn than from the stars themselves!

Autism is not the end state- it's the journey to recovery through relentless intervention, research and support.

Hopefully this will give families and people with Autism an invaluable insight and renewed hope into how to manage and perhaps even cure Autism and/or reduce the impact of Autism in their lives.

1. What is Autism?
2. My brother; God made him perfect
3. What could cause Autism?
4. So your brother/sister/cousin etc. has Autism; where do we go from here?
5. Dos and Don'ts
6. Having faith and belief that healing is possible!

Enjoy peeps!

WHAT IS AUTISM?

Autism Spectrum Disorder (ASD) is a developmental disability. It commonly presents itself in early childhood, however some individuals may not be diagnosed until later. ASD is a collective spectrum of behaviours, physical, neurological and psychological that result in social withdrawal and blurred vision of the world. That is my best definition and understanding of Autism thus far although the exact behaviour ASD is a continuum, some individuals may have mild presentation, living independent lives, and others may have more severe disabilities requiring continued support and care. [1] Autism is real and it's devastatingly hard but the rewards and peace one receives both from someone autistic and in helping them is unimaginably greater and more rewarding than the hardship itself that it lead me to believe that recovery through Jesus is possible. God created our brother in this way for a reason; to change us, to make us value life itself more and to see God's glory through him through belief that Yoseph could be healed.

According to Holly Bridges 'Reframe your thinking around Autism'- a brilliant book I recommend that opens the reader's mind as autism being workable and child can retrain their brain to become better and heal. Holly Bridges defines autism as 'in Academic research community, autism is discussed as a brain disorder with a genetic basis. Yet no specific biomarker can diagnoses autism as of yet'.

The book introduces a new theory for autism first defined by Dr Stephen Porges 'The Polyvagal Theory', poly meaning many and Vagal referring to the vagal nerve.

Dr Stephen Porges argues that the vagus nerve is a cranial nerve that conveys sensory information about the state of the body to the nervous system. 'The body has two systems. One runs up and down with the body and brain, communicating how things are. When things are running smoothly, things are bi-directional; The other system goes round and rolls through various organisms in the abdomen.'[12]

When we detect a threat, the Poly vague theory states that our new vagus system, which relies on external information to be conveyed to our body and brain, turns to 'fight or flight' response; all thenergy that was used in flowing around the body is blocked. Dr Porges thinks that many autistic are people for whom, as infants, their vagal system was diverted to the body's fight or flight mode and has stayed in this form. The theory is centred on the idea that body and brain are interconnected and opens the door that our brains and in turn bodies can be retrained to move away from this panic state to becoming open to the 'social engagement system'[12].

Autism is not only a developmental disability; it is a neurological and emotional disability that causes children and adults to perceive the world in a disorganised way and the inability to process information, sounds, language in a coherent manner causes great distress.

Autism is strongly linked to genetic factors. As our understanding of the human genome increases, we are able to identify genetic markers which may result in autism. For different conditions – for example cystic fibrosis – the genetic markers are clear. With autism, there seems to be a range of genetic markers which may produce autism, but which do not invariably produce autism. As an example, there are cases of identical twins where one twin has autism and the other does not. The current thinking, therefore, is that autism results from a combination of a genetic difference and one or more environmental factors.[11]

Delay, Repetition and Social Withdrawal

A utism is a continuous spectrum of various traits and behaviours that can be typified as being delayed, repetitive and socially withdrawn.

Delay means a delay in speech, academic work, and developing milestones like learning how to ride a bike. Also, delay in understanding social rules for example to say 'hello' and 'goodbye' to a person, to look both ways when crossing the road, to not stare. It's amazing though how many people forget to do the same to the autistic child! Once the child understands, they can't stop! My brother came to the point where he was saying hello to strangers on the street, some replying with warmth and admiration others more stunned and likes say gob-smacked.

Delay in speech usually arises in the first 3 years of the child's life and can either be overcome or a small percentage of autistic people remain essentially non-verbal to adulthood. 'Whereas about half of all preverbal children with ASD become verbally fluent by the time they enter nursery, the other half have significant delays, with about 30% remaining "minimally verbal" (fewer than 20 functional, flexible words; per consensus terminology of the National Institutes of Health workshop)[4]'[5]

Studies find that younger children make greater progress in intervention than older children, although the reasons for this are not completely clear[5]. This might be because the brain in a younger child is more 'elastic' so to speak and so has a higher capacity to gather more skills in the same time than for an older child, although I believe ultimately our brain capacity in both cases is infinite- there is no limit to how much we can learn and know!

I want to stress that you should never look purely at the language abilities of a child when looking at their ability to progress in life; just because a child does not speak does not mean that they do not think, process and want the ability to communicate. Quite the opposite sometimes; these children are more desperate than ever to get their message across but the reason they can't is because it's difficult for them. So please do not lose hope on a non-verbal child; there are times when I see a non-verbal autistic adult and whilst of course I cannot pose judgement, I believe that if someone had believed in this person more when they were a child there could have been some verbal communication in adult life.

Repetition is the continual repeating of certain behaviour patterns for example repeating the same word again and again. If the child hears a word and continuously repeats it, the formal word for this is 'Echolalia'. Echolalia is a form of imitation. Imitation is a useful, normal and necessary component of social learning: *imitative learning* occurs when the "observer acquires new behaviours through imitation" and *mimicry* or *automatic imitation* occurs when a "re-enacted behaviour is based on previously acquired motor (or vocal) patterns". [3]

Echolalia is used my many autistic children, partially to sustain a conversation when the ability to produce spontaneous speech is difficult (autistic children very often have many concurrent thoughts and ideas in their minds simultaneously and sometimes they are drawn to having the same thought repeat over and over again in their heads- for example Yoseph will often have a specific car in his mind that might have reminded him of something and he repeats the name over and over again).

Social withdrawal is the inability to communicate with people, in the case of an autistic person, either due to lack of eye contact, speech or awareness of the importance of it. Social withdrawal is in a way an inevitable consequence of autism because it is so difficult for neuro-typical children and adults to empathise let alone understand the hardship of what the autistic person is going through, they are often isolated from their peers. It is a serious problem because social withdrawal can ultimately lead to loneliness and lack of social connection heightens health risks as much as smoking 15 cigarettes a day or having alcohol use disorder. She's also found that loneliness and social isolation are twice as harmful to physical and mental health as obesity [6]. Social withdrawal is the most obvious and yet the most subtle out of all the symptoms; there is a risk of it going under the radar as it did in Yoseph's case. This is partly because autistic children can sometimes be very socially withdrawn and in other instances, may show great yearning to interact with a person. Consistency is key and very often the missing puzzle piece. Social interaction encompasses any form of communication designed to engage another person e.g. gestures, hand movements, signalling and verbal speech. There must be active steps taken to help your child integrate in some form with their peers even be it saying hello and goodbye twice a day to two different children; playing with sandcastles in the park with other children so they feel a sense of belonging. This is very important.

One vital point to make note of in autism which is that no-one child/adult can be typified by a conventional developmental timeline; in that there is no consistent development course [10] in Autistic people; some may grow to become world renowned maths professors, others may work in Starbucks and struggle on a daily basis to hold the cups with a fine grip. What is important and certain though is that autistic children/adults need to be aware of their strengths and a support system needs to prevail so as to allow them to make a contribution to this world; they are humans just like us and they understand and yearn to leave the world a better place than when they first set foot here!

Communication

Swinburne University of Technology has shared a 'person first approach' to Autism where the person puts themselves in the shoes of the Autistic person, with the hope of better understanding the experiences of that person. A core principle of achieving this person first approach is effective communication. Communication is singularly the most significant barrier to bettering the lives of Autistic people. It is the lack of communication with Autistic people that stops us from understanding the hopes, the fears and the difficulties these people face in their lives- it leads to build up of frustration, anxiety and also inhibits us from noticing the joy in the Autistic people when they experience it. They may not shout and laugh and beam as we do when joyous but this does certainly not mean they are not joyful! They may flap their arms instead or tap on a metallic surface- the acoustics of the surface in harmony with their frequency of joy.

A core principle is awakening interest in the child/adult and trying to find common ground as well as responding to any sounds/ technologies they use to communicate. This builds motivation for the Autistic person because their yearning to communicate is already there!

Can do approach

It is very important to have a 'can do' approach for children with Autism rather than 'I can't'. Many autistic people already have negative connotations of their Autism due to stigma attached to it and the stereotypes built by society so they may have a default 'I can't' attitude. Help to change this around to 'I can'- I can play with this toy, I can learn how to speak in full sentences one day etc. We all have talents and dreams and if these are celebrated in a positive way and encouraged through motivation, hard work and encouragement, autistic people can go far with their dreams.

This can be applied on a small scale at home e.g. when helping to clean in the kitchen. The child may have sensitivity to the smell of ketchup and clearing it up may be difficult but if you encourage the child that they CAN do it, then one day they may attempt to clear it. This small scale positivity will transcend into greater ventures in life and reflect the change in mind set.

Autistic people are surprisingly more positive than we are about their Autism- they see it as only part of them and do not allow their difficulties to stop them from embracing life; the very least we can do is help support them!

Meltdowns

Meltdowns are one of the least discussed areas of Autism that have profound emotional, psychological and physical impact on the lives of people with Autism and their loved ones. It can be emotionally scarring and their occurrence and intensity varies greatly although I believe all people with Autism experience meltdowns and although their cause and intensity is very often beyond control, it is at their most vulnerable state that we can experience the humanness of a person with Autism and see the core of their fears. My brother sometimes has meltdowns before entering a loud shopping centre, before a young child comes near him for fear the child may scream and he loses complete control. This manifests itself in visible shaking, gridding of teeth and an acute period of intense anxiety. It is heartbreaking to see it happen, let alone find a method to intervene so as to minimise the risk of harm happening to that child. It is important to acknowledge its presence and have mechanisms ready to help the child e.g. have 'chewy' toys to help the child bite instead of the child biting themselves, putting on soft, damping gloves to absorb the shock of any punches they may through.

Meltdowns encapsulate a true snapshot of when a child with Autism's coping mechanisms fail and their resilience drops to zero. Resilience is the ability to bounce back after a challenging situation and I believe meltdowns help to build the resilience of the child more and more. Meltdowns usually occur when the child's coping strategies fail so the key to avoid meltdowns is:

- Avoid throwing your child in the deep end without notice e.g. taking them to a loud shopping centre if they can't handle it
- Build resilience step by step; e.g. take your child to a small shopping centre or at an early hour when there are not many people. The child will see they CAN be ok, and that will build their coping mechanism and resilience.

This will allow the child to stay in stressful situations longer and more successful until one day they may be able to be there for the entire time without any anxiety! Patience combined with coping strategies will help the child make this significant step in their lives; not be overwhelmed by their surroundings and have a meltdown. Meltdowns can still inevitably occur from time to time; we cannot predict every situation where there could disturbing noises but what we can have at the ready is a coping strategy to minimise the impact and help the child feel safe.

Why do autistic people experience sensory sensitivities?

Statistics show from the Autism Alliance that over 90% of people with Autism experience sensory difficulties. Sensory processing refers to how your mind and body process information obtained from the five key senses. Most 'normal' people are able to perceive and respond to information obtained from their sense of smell, sound, sight, touch and taste immediately without an imbalance in processing and response; we take these things for granted for example smelling the scent of a delicate, blossoming lavender plant, hearing the screeching siren of an ambulance; although some of these stimuli may be overwhelming even for ourselves, our body has the ability to detect the loudness of the sound and because of our immediate processing we are able to respond accordingly e.g. move away from the ambulance so as to reduce the sound. Autistic people differ in many ways.

Autistic people will normally sense an under stimulation or over stimulation and as a result this lead to lack of awareness that the stimuli is actually present or oversensitivity and a desire to move away from what in our perception is a nominally quiet/medium sound. Secondly, their delay in processing the information may cause them to respond at a delayed time e.g. after an ambulance has driven past. More catasphorically, they sometimes build up the information gathered and it is processed in one big go that may become overwhelming for them; this can lead to what we call a 'meltdown'.

Autistic people can be over- or under-sensitive to any of their senses including: Touch, Sound, Sight, Taste, Smell, Balance (vestibular) and awareness of where your body is in space (proprioception).[11]

There is no simple cause of Autism unlike other conditions and there is huge biological research that needs to be done on genetics and also social interactions and reducing the 'stigma' of Autism to help Autistic people interact more and take a more welcoming and active role in society. Also, including the views and experiences of Autistic people is a key aspect to making groundbreaking progress in our understanding but also in healing of autism.

Language used towards Autistic people

High functioning vs. low functioning

Autistic people are not on or the other; they usually exemplify a combination of both.

Making the most of strengths

Autistic people very often have spiked profiles; meaning they have great strengths in certain skills in their life and have difficulty in others. While this may pose a challenge to day to day living, we can firstly identify what the strength is (it might be a memory for names or ability to conduct multiple calculations simultaneously or have a profound visual memory), it is about harnessing it next and finding a methodology that will allow the child to use this strength for example if a child has great memory for names they might consider a future career in teaching, learning support or perhaps even authoring maps with all the towns and villages in England. They might also work as a tour guide for remembrance of key names and dates is an essential prerequisite to this profession. On a shorter term note, they may be given responsibility at home to write a list of family and friends to send a Christmas message to.

People with Autism are amazing human beings, their perception of the world, although unusual and unfamiliar, is unbiased, non-judgemental, takes great joy in small things and has an incredible level of detail entwined in it. Making most of their strengths is something that, with planning and empathy, can have long-lasting implications. A key element is to define their strengths, assess the context in which they need to used, foster motivation and have support mechanism in place to help the child/adult to flourish in their setting.

An example is my brother Yoseph who has incredible attention to detail and enjoys doing 'spot the difference' where two images are shown with very subtle differences. I have used this in teaching my brother chemical reactions specifically acid and metal reactions and acid and alkali reactions. He has been given the two chemical equation and asked to 'spot the difference'- Yoseph has a passion for Science and this combined with the 'spot the difference' accelerated his learning and we combined both passions into one! It can be challenging to apply this to day to day activities; always keep the happiness and well-being of the child/adult as the pivotal focus and you will find a solution!

Mark Carney, founder of the 'I CAN Network' and an Aspergers states that there are four key characteristics that are prevalent in most people with Autism and they are 'amazing memory, attention to detail, visual perception and their incredible ability to focus'. [13]

Leveraging their strengths will give them a voice in the World and make a valuable contribution to society. Make the time to develop the person's strengths on a regular basis for example ask a child to read their favourite book if they have great reading skills, puzzles if they have great attention to detail or paint a scene they saw during the day to develop their memory skills.

Some existing intervention methods

JASPER

Kasari's research focuses on targeted interventions for early social communication development in at-risk infants, toddlers, and preschoolers with autism, and peer relationships for school-aged children with autism. Kasari has led several randomized controlled trials of therapeutic interventions for children with autism. Her team developed Joint Attention Symbolic Play Engagement and Regulation (JASPER) therapy as an evidence-based treatment for autistic children.[11][12] JASPER aims to improve joint engagement, social communication, and emotion regulation, and decrease child negativity, while improving parental co-regulation strategies

Son-Rise program

Son-Rise is a home-based program for children and adults with autism spectrum disorders and other developmental disabilities, which was developed by Barry Neil Kaufman and Samahria Lyte Kaufman for their son Raun, who was diagnosed with autism and is claimed to have fully recovered from his condition.[1] The program is described by Autism Speaks as a "child-centered program that places parents as the key therapists and directors of their program."[2][medical citation needed]

AAC

(AUGMENTATIVE AND ALTERNATIVE COMMUNICATION)

Children with learning disabilities (including Autism but also conditions such as Down's Syndrome et.c) want to communicate with their loved ones- there is evidence of this and contrary to our models of autism, autistic people sometimes make sounds to actually communicate and their lack of eye contact is not because they do not want to communicate but don't know how.

Augmentative and alternative communication encompasses communication methods use to supplement or replace speech or writing for those with impairments in the production of spoken or written language. AAC is used by those with autism. The symbols used in AAC include gestures, photographs, pictures, line drawings, letters and words which can be used along or in combination. [7]

Neurotypicals communicate in a code called language that is often illogical: we often don't mean what we say or say what we mean. Neurotypicals assume that *context* is as relevant to meaning as actual words, so to ascertain the real meaning of language, a degree of empathising is necessary. [9]

I like and agree with the point that neuro-typicals communicate in a language where we don't mean what we say and just because autistic people are not showing 'emphathy' (they might be bored or not understand a given situation or how a person is feeling) does not mean they do not emphathise!

[8] Communication board is an AAC method that is low-tech.

Impact of Autism on families and loved ones

Autism, regardless of the severity, presents the child/adult with an unexplainable suffering caused by lack of understanding, sensory overload and uncertainty of the future. Appreciation and empathy is the first key step towards building a lifelong relationship with a person with Autism. Autistic people, contrary to popular belief and research, want to build relationships and trust. I can tell from firsthand experience with my dear brother who's spent the last 10 years trying to explain to me why he doesn't like using the London Overground train; if he wasn't interested in building a connection, surely he would have stopped by now? Motivation is fundamental and with an appropriate *means* to communicate, communication is then the product.

Autism is a highly variable, individualised development disorder whose symptoms first appear during infancy or childhood and generally follows a steady course without remission. [2] Dependency on family members and loved ones must never be underestimated; children and adults with autism often are challenged with completing simple and minute day to day tasks from brushing their teeth, cooking food and being able to interact in a safe, coherent manner with the outside world. It is essential that loved ones can if possible get as early a diagnosis as possible should be completed.

Diagnosis is often completed once a set of verbal/communication/developmental delays have been observed and the advice of specialists has been sought. Of course, the reality is far from as simple and usually a recurring of this cycle must take place between 2-5 times, where the symptoms are discussed with a variety of specialists. Sometimes, one specialist will give a unanimous decision that the child/adult has autism; sometimes it is an agreed yet uncertain decision that the child does (unofficially) have autism. The former is beneficial in the sense that first family members, however devastating the news is, have the peace in knowing the prognosis of their child and can apply to get an EHC plan for school (an Educational, Health and Care plan where the needs of the child and the underlying support required n class are explicitly detailed).

Children who are undiagnosed do not have the basis in which their parents can apply for in class support in school and obtain a paediatrician (although the effectiveness of your doctor can be based on what borough/state you live in- for example my brother was assigned a paediatrician and she was completely unresponsive to his need of peeing frequently at night!)

Having said this, Autistic people also are the most joyful people in the World because they marvel and see the Goodness in small things that we take for granted. When they are able to answer a question in the first go, for example, or consume an ice-cream that previously felt like something slithering down their throat for the first time, there is a wonderful, inexplicable and triumphant joy in them that spreads like a mighty river of fresh water. A happy autistic child/adult can bring light to not only a room but to an entire city!

Autistic people often show a sensitivity to smell, sound and taste. This is great simplification of a complex disability but taking notice of these sensitivities is a vital and useful step in building a relationship with an Autistic person; remember empathy!

Autistic people want:

- Love; Love is the epitome of life and the more we love, the more love we will receive back from our children
- Nurturing; they want to learn and understand the world around and their sensory and emotional difficulties prevents them from doing so
- Loyalty
- Eternal relationships; Autistic people are not in this for fake, temporary friendships/relationships, they're in for the real thing! Unlike many of us, they understand that good everlasting relationships require patience and time.

Autism- why it is so hard?

My brother; God made him perfect

My brother (whose name I exempt for privacy) born on 10th January 2003 in London. Mum had a joyful, amazing and every increasing painful pregnancy; he was safely delivered 10 days after the due date. Yoseph was a ray of sunshine in our life; he was the missing puzzle. He gave us the opportunity to be young again and having been 10 years of age at the time, I felt a strong responsibility and mother-like instinct towards my youngest sibling. He was happy, beautiful, smiley boy who loved catapulting Ready Brek porridge across the kitchen. His record was 1.5m. My brother enjoyed doing puzzles and he marvelled at the wonders of nature and cinema; he has a particular taste for fine foods and he enjoyed building, play-doughing, reading books and going for long drives. To be honest, looking back at my brother of 3 months, there was no sign of abnormality; the idea of disability never even crossed my mind because no-one in my family as far as I knew ever even had a disability. It was something that you say in strangers for example a person in a wheelchair, a person with Downs Syndrome; you sympathise and gave blessing but you knew it wasn't part of your life so you didn't really give it a second thought.

The only subtle anomaly was that by the age of 9 months, he was not producing any sounds. We assumed like every family does; it will 'happen'. He's probably slightly delayed, lets give him some time. Time is the essence of life right; only time can tell. But as time ticks, and life evolves, children grow up, exams are passed, new destinations are discovered but my brother was still not producing any sounds. So we kept going with life whilst having this, for the very first time, an uneasy uncertain thought at the back of our minds that Yoseph is 'special'. What this meant for us, we did not know yet. The next step was toe-walking and this was abnormal- this confirmed it wasn't just a speech delay or such.

God help us! Was the first thought in our head when a doctor in Poland first suggested He had autism. The whos, how, where and what was completely a mystery at the present moment in time. Yoseph was now three years of age and about to start the greatest journey through school. He was still non-verbal and a few what we now recognise as sensory symptoms arose; toe-walking, sensitivity to sounds and cries of fear. We account this to be 'misbehaviour' but its still a cry for help.

Diagnosis is very important because you need to understand the link between the symptoms that child/adult are displaying, and access correct help to manage the symptoms. What is tragic still for so many autistic people is that lack of support they obtain from local authorities and schools.

How my brother went through nursery and Reception without the ability to verbally communicate is one of the greatest modern mysteries and wonders and made my attainment of As and A*s at GCSE seem incredibly miniature in comparison, like an elephant standing side by side with an ant. I was still young at the time and didn't quite understand it all; it resonated with 'dyslexia' or something similar; one of those labels teachers, professionals and doctors use to typify certain behaviours. The reason stemmed from my lack of familiarity of autism; it was unheard of when I came to school. I knew one thing; my little baby brother was disadvantaged, he needed our help with every great might we could give and I would do anything to protect my little brother from harm as he made his way through this amazing yet dangerous world.

Until the age of approximately three, my brother didn't display many symptoms typified by autism. For example, he had strong eye contact, was able to walk on his feet and didn't flap his arms. These are very often early indicators that a child/adult may have autism and is typified by restless, inconsistent and apprehensive behaviour. He did however cry when subject to loud sounds (this was not immediately identified at the time) and ate only a limited range of foods which had significant implications on his health. He yearned for high wheat-content foods such as pasta and pizza which are said to have an adverse effect on the neurology of autistic people. The most obvious indicator was that he was non-verbal. In a sense these early years of living in uncertainty and lack of clarity where the most difficult for me as a sister because whilst I wanted to do a great many journeys, story-telling, riding the bike, playing hide and seek with my brother I had this underlying and overwhelming feeling that this was not going to be quite so possible. Or maybe it was, and I had to wait and see.

As a baby, it is a natural stage of progression in growth that a child begins to take active steps towards verbal communication beginning with parents. My brother did not produce hardly any sounds and up to the age of three he communicated with two main words 'ow' which meant 'out, going outside' and 'D' which meant 'DVD' because he enjoyed films. All other form of communication was in the form of hand gestures, 'eh' to indicate he wanted something .it was a very frustrating and agonising time, both for himself and Mum and all of us, because Yoseph wanted to communicate so desperately and yet was unable to. Sometimes the more we prompted the more frustrated he became.

His inability to make friends and the lack of support in school was also very difficult to consume; although the children in his class were lovely, good children who tolerated him and accepted him, there was no active steps on our part and the school's part to help Yoseph integrate with his peers; this breaks my heart writing this now. We must do things better in the future.

It is difficult to put into words when it dawns that your brother may not have as easy a life as you. You love your sibling/child with all your might, more than yourself and so the prospect that they will have to suffer and at the certain moment in time, you have no power (or at least you think you have no power) to change it is unbearable and overwhelming. It was a time of intense self-reflection, where I looked back at the choices I made in my life and saw how easy things were for me. Why did I ever complain about my periods and GCSES?! Well, the periods yes but GCSEs- I had the ability to complete them independently and to rejoice with friends when I Passed; Lord how selfish I was! I was in control of myself and there were no neurological and physical barriers to stop me from conquering the world. I knew with God's help that my brother would make it in life but I had no platform to build this tiny grain of faith on. It needed water and how the quest was to find this source of water that would help Yoseph grow so he too could blossom, learn and make a difference in the world.

The first stage of teaching my brother to speak was the speech therapy sessions. This was challenging not least how to fund the cost but to find a therapist who could teach a child who did not understand yet the power of communication, not simply a child who had difficulty making sentences. This was a whole new level.

We searched far and wide and used a combination of three techniques all of which will be detailed in this book; The Son Rise Program, conventional speech therapy and physical exercises to improve the flow of neurone signals in the spine. I believe that these three, with God's help helped my brother speak and without the input of our family (primarily our Mother),speech therapists, teachers our little brother would not have spoken so thank you to all of you.

My brother first started going to a private speech therapist when he was (please check the year) and also to occupational therapy at the Centre in London. Unfortunately this faculty has closed but it was a charity run organisation that aimed at improving the education and health of disabled children. It had a reliable, competent and passionate team of professionals some of whom worked with my brother for several years. One lady who made a great impact was Debbie Grey, a brilliant Teacher who taught my brother Maths and English. Although I never saw Debbie teach my brother in person, a video showed a teacher who instilled discipline and calmness into my brother's learning, something that was lacking abundantly and a skill that most teachers who worked with him did not possess. This was my first prerequisites lesson as a Teacher that calmness and willingness to learn is first and foremost before any teaching can take place.

Our Mother and Father have been through a journey beyond words . It is said that parents often notice signs in the first three years of the child's life. [2] I think this was the case with my brother. The difficult part is being truthful to yourself in recognising these signs; often we dismiss these signs as 'oh, he will grow up', 'he still has time to learn', 'its probably a phase; the speech therapist will sort him out'. But unless we take the first action in recognising the signs, there is no way we can ACT upon them and take crucial and active steps in managing and reducing Autism.

So, fast forwarding into time (I will discuss how we manage holidays, sleeping, learning, going to work, finishing Oxford, graduations, teaching and bus driving all later), my brother is 19 years old and is attending a College which he is immensely proud and happy to be a part of. My brother can now speak in simple to highly developed sentences and he thoroughly enjoys learning English, Maths, Science, painting, watching films, going to the gym with his classmates and has spoken of dreams to become a teacher in a specialist school. As far as social interactions are concerned praise God he has come a long way to the point where he sometimes stops strangers in the train stations and asks what their name is! Making friends is still a major obstacle but he has made some friends in his old school and we are determined and committed to helping him make one friend with whom he can connect with on a social, emotional and psychological level, someone with whom he can confide in without judgement or fear and someone who has empathy and understands what he has to go through each day.

We love our brother very very very much and through the meltdowns, the tears, the rejoicing moments when Yoseph made his first sentence, to the insomniac nights to all the moments of laughter, we wouldn't have made this journey any different to what it is and of course we are going towards gold; a true Healing from the Almighty. Because in healing our brother we too are being healed.

So your brother/sister/cousin etc. has Autism; where do we go from here?

So you have received the news you were dreading; your son/daughter/sister/brother/cousin has autism. This means a long struggle with speech, with acceptance, with managing stimulation and behaviour and always being different from others. Now for the GOOD News; this is your chance to grow with your child whilst you find ways to heal him and help function at home, help his/her eating patterns, sleeping, making friends and helping him/her have a place in this world. You must believe truly in your hearts that through your loved one's disability, God will manifest His Greatness in them by healing them. I believe this is the Truth and I believe that one day my brother will be healed from autism.

With this belief comes your conviction; that change is possible. Whilst we must love and accept our brother as he is and embrace and adapt our lives right now, we can steer him/her towards change through consistent support both at home and from professionals and provide 'windows' of 'normality' where he/she can see what its like to experience 'normality' without feeling overwhelmed. It's a

Anxiety is inevitably a key part of Autism both for the child/adult and family members. Anxiety, in my opinion, should not be seen as a mental illness the same way as schrophrenia; it is a state of mind.

Intellectual disability vs. Autism

The diagnosis of intellectual and developmental disabilities is based on three criteria:

- All the issues are present before the age of 18
- There is a significant impairment in intellectual ability (typically an IQ score below 70)
- There is a significant requirement for support in everyday life[9]

It is a common conception that children with autism are more likely to have an intellectual disability in that not only do they have sensory problems but also find it difficult to process information and have significant requirement for support. Intellectual disability is often associated with a delay in key milestones such as walking, talking, washing their own hands etc. I challenge this viewpoint that because Autistic people require support because of sensory and processing needs, this does not necessarily mean they are 'slow' intellectually; for example an autistic child may already know the answer to 5+10 a second after asking but if they don't possess the ability to SAY it, it may seem they are intellectually 'disabled' .

DOS AND DON'TS

Sleeping

utistic people (both adults and children) experience to some extent difficulty sleeping. Here are some tragedies that may help your child sleep

- Glass of milk before bedtime
- Toilet before sleep to empty the bladder
- Avoid large meals after 7pm-digestion will occur later and disrupt sleep.
- Avoid screens.
- Make sure there are no strong smells/lights near vicinity of room. E.g. after smell of fast food
- Make sure the room is cool for sleeping

Many autistic children (perhaps adults in some cases) find themselves with difficulty controlling their bowel movement. Their peeing is irregular and I believe due to sensory difficult a child with autism may not have the sensation when to go to the loo as we do. Constipation and irregular peeing is something to be very alert to as children can sometimes forget to go to the loo- this can be dangerous. The child may have a bladder full of pee but not feel the urge to go to the loo- this is called under-sensitivity. Then we they fall asleep they pee themselves and this, of course, causes them great discomfort and pain and may disturb their sleep.

It is excruciating work for the parents too who are awake with their child during this difficult time. Parents are tired, exhausted physically and emotionally from seeing their child in pain. This can bring long-term stress and its importance to seek help where necessary. Explain clearly to the class teacher if and when your child has not slept well as it may affect their alertness, irritability and safety.

Please consult your GP about the urination each day.

TEACHING AN AUTISTIC CHILD

Many autistic children (if not all) require extra support at school and home with their academic learning. It is important to recognise this early and intervene. Although it can be overwhelming with a prospect of having to teach your child the entire Curriculum, taking small and purposeful steps is key. To understand more complex structures in English, be able to apply models in Science and master compare and contrasting poems in Essay writing requires learning of basic skills first.

Teach your child the basics first; even if this takes a long time, is repetitive to an extent, make sure the foundation is strong. Autistic people struggle to create models in their head and link learnt knowledge to solving a problem, particularly when the problem has to be visualised. For example, one may teach 4+5=9 but what does 4 represent? If you ask the child to add 4 apples with 5 apples, its important to demonstrate through a physical model so your child can 'see' the number 4 and the number 5. The next step is to count all the apples together- suddenly the four and five together becomes nine. This is quite an abstract concept that requires many parts of the brain to wire together to make this deduction. Practice is next. Once you've practiced, one can say the child has gained some mastery.

Little successes with the autistic child reap huge rewards and in the journey of teaching the child, it becomes a journey of self-discovery, resilience and joy for you too. Make sure you have different methods of modelling at the ready with your child, for example coins, flash cards to introduce sentence starters/structures e.g. 'I can', 'You can','They can'. Use these and experiment with them to build sentences. Once you have modelled

The process can be as follows:

Introduce concept
Model the concept to your child.

Model the concept through example

E.g. frying an egg is an example of a chemical reaction.

Give a real life example

e.g. mixing lemon juice with bicarbonate with soda is an example of neutralisation

Your child models the concept

Ask your child to do the example. For example to write

Practice applying the concept

Teaching strategies

Technology can play a very helpful tool in teaching an autistic child; bright colours and interesting videos can help stimulate interest and activate parts of the brain from the stimuli and open receptors to learning new information. Notice the use of the word tool; do not use an iPad to teach the whole lesson on adding numbers from 1-10 but use it as an aid perhaps to show a simulation of adding 4 apples to 3 apples. Technology can become over reliant as we rely on a PowerPoint presentation to 'teach' the children the lesson; this can make the teacher and in turn the children passive as you feel like you are teaching quite literally from a screen. Remember communication as well as teacher knowledge is key to learning for children and teaching from you first and using the PowerPoint to give examples/visual aids as an aid comes second.

As a Science teacher, technology can be useful in presenting new information and showing animations of physical models e.g. how the Earth rotates around the Sun. Begin by introducing a new concept through a very simple explanation e.g. the Earth rotates once every 365 days a year. Then provide a worksheet that helps the child consolidate their understanding- do not present new knowledge on the worksheet as it can confuse the child.

e.g. her is an extract from a PowerPoint slide on the Earth, Moon and Sun. Very simple slide with minimal information and succinct explanation. Then proceed by asking your child 'how long is year'. Targeted questioning is important.

Proceed by offering for example a multiple choice quiz with questions based on the lesson e.g. how long is one year a)300 days b)365 days c)400 days. Try to make the choices viable but also differentiable so the child can identify the correct answer. E.g. no point doing a) 364 b)365.5 c)365.6

Earth and the Sun

The Earth travels around the sun every 365 and ¼ days which we call a year.

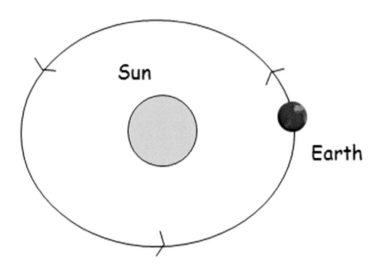

Remember to teach little and often, use as little distraction in your teaching as possible. Abstract concepts must be explained in a clear manner as Autistic people learn things literally and teach the core principles in the most plain, clear way as possible. Avoid use of too many sounds and wording but rather define important definitions and explain the concept in a few sentences. Use of media such as videos to illustrate and develop understanding is helpful.

Assessments

I am super super proud to say that my brother has reached the academic stage and level of concentration that he was able to pass his first set of qualifications in 2019- Entry Level Certificate in English and Maths and he is now working towards the AQA Entry Level Certificate in Science. Exam technique is both powerful and challenging to master as it requires from the user concentration, focus, determination and a calm demeanour.

REFERENCES [1]

https://www.brainwave.org.uk/
autism?gclid=CjwKCAiA1rPyBRAREiwA1UIy8BKuvmpjwS3o6tu42sm
gQlgVAfgSlQPkzkhPuLFvBhz2MKr4JC_7hoCh6gQAvD_BwE

https://transformingautism.org/struggle/?gclid=EAIaIQobChMIsY3hury46AIVQ
bTtCh3Rigw-EAAYASAAEgKlyfD_BwE

[2] Wikipedia- Autism

[3] Ganos C, Ogrzal T, Schnitzler A, Münchau A (September 2012). «The pathophysiology of echopraxia/echolalia: relevance to Gilles de la Tourette syndrome». *Mov. Disord.* **27** (10): 1222–9. doi:10.1002/mds.25103. PMID 22807284.

[4] Tager-Flusberg & Kasari, 2013),

National Institute on Deafness and Other Communication Disorders, 2010;

[5] Kasari et. Al SMARTer Approach to Personalizing Intervention for Children With Autism Spectrum Disorder

[6] Julianne Holt-Lunstad *Perspectives on Psychological Science*, Vol. 10, No. 2, 2015).

[7] Wikipedia 'Augmentative and Alternative communication'

[8] Quadell, Self-made sample page from a low-tech w:Augmentative and alternative communication aid 2011

[9] Future Learn; 'Understanding Autism' University of Kent

[10] Future Learn; 'Understanding Autism' University of Kent

[11] https://www.autism-alliance.org.uk/autism-f-a-qs/

[12] Holly Bridges 'Reframe your thinking around Autism'

[13] Mark Carney 'I CAN Network'

According to Dr. Karen Guldberg, there is a discrepancy between what autistic people believe is good for them vs. what research says. This is the basis of evidence based practice. We should not privilege research evidence opposed to professional evidence. How can practice contribute to the scientific knowledge base

ABOUT THE AUTHOR

No dream is too big. Not even if you have autism.

Through frustrations, speech delay, lack of friends, persistent judgements against all odds this book describes what it means to find success as an autistic person- through the eyes of a sister!

Printed in the United States
by Baker & Taylor Publisher Services